"Doggy Tails"

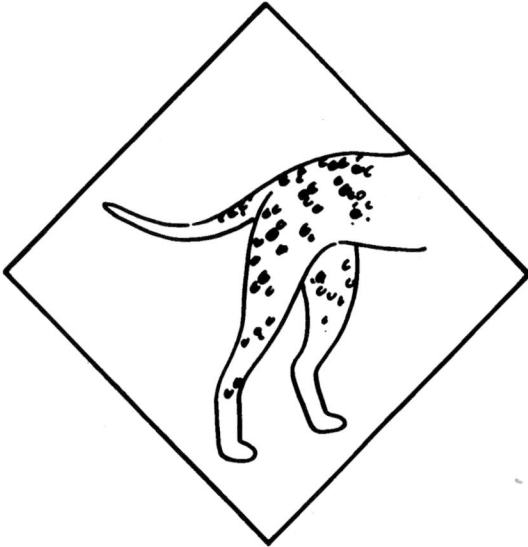

a collection of

poems for dog and puppy lovers

Created, Edited and Produced 1998 Sylvia Barnes
Text 1998 © Glenda Ramsay (contributor Sylvia Barnes)
Illustrations © 1998 Anita Lawrence
Cover Design © 1998 Helen Roe
This edition © K2 Koncepts Ltd.

First Edition 1999

Published by K2 Koncepts Ltd
PO Box 1713
Fordingbridge
Hants
SP6 3RZ

E-Mail: k2.koncepts@btinternet.com

ISBN 1 902968 00 X

Printed and Bound in Christchurch, Dorset, United Kingdom
by Bargates Print and Design - Tel: 01202 480009

...............Contents...............

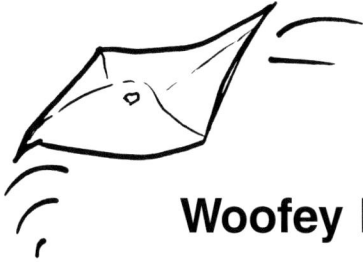

Woofey Dog Tails

He raced round the garden
He charged up and down stairs
He chewed up the curtains
And the legs of the chairs.
He played with the kitten
And chased his red ball.
He woofed at his reflection
In the mirror in the hall.
He did love his walkies
Especially in the rain.
He always got dirty
He drove me insane.
Each morning in a frenzy
I'd rush to the door
To reach for the letters as they fell to the floor.
If he found them before me
He'd have such a good time
Scattering the letters
Oh! what a pantomime.
He could be so naughty
And then Oh! so good.
He did make me laugh though
But then all puppies should.

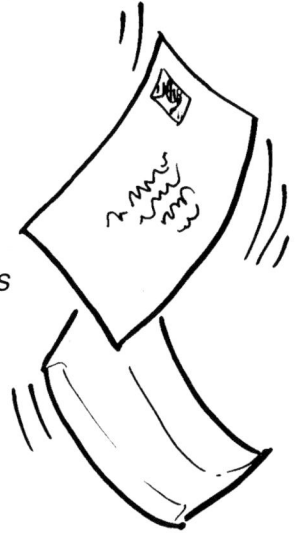

The Runaway

I found him sitting outside my door
He looked so sad as he gave me his paw.
His big brown eyes pleaded
They said, please let me stay
From my other home I've run away.
I gave him some dinner and a long cold drink
He had been on the run some days I think.
His coat was all matted and he looked quite thin
And he smelt just like an old dustbin.
After I'd bathed him and made him smell nice
A great big lick meant he'd found paradise.
The days went by and he still wasn't claimed
So the time had come for him to be named.
He had long silky hair and a big bushy beard
He looked so different from the day he appeared.
He had chosen to stay so now he's mine
We go for long walks in the warm sunshine.
He always obeys me when he's called
So I decided to call my new dog......Ozwald!

Silver the Greyhound

Silver ran fast
And never came last
Harry was slow
With no get up and go
Silver will win
Because she's so thin
Harry's never a winner
Co's he eats too much dinner!

Doris the Dachshund

Sometimes she's sad if she's called a sausage
For this little dog has lots of courage.
She has a long body close to the ground
Her name is Doris and she's a Dachshund.
In the rain she'll splash in the puddles
Even though it comes up to her middle.
She has two bright little eyes
That are full of surprise.
From her nose to her tail she looks so sweet
With her four short legs and four tiny feet.
She'll come at once when you call her name
And is always ready for a game.
After her dinner she'll feel quite complete
And fall asleep on the rug by your feet.

Blind Dogs

Golden Retrievers are very kind
Some are taught to lead the blind.
They guide them carefully along the street
Always there but very discreet.
A faithful, loving, gentle friend
Your life, with his, he will defend.
Their instinct for safety is superb
They'll halt their owner at the kerb.
They look right and left, before crossing with pride
And when it's safe they boldly stride.
Many miles with their owners' they'll roam
But they always lead them safely home.
Together they will always be
Because their owner's cannot see.

Working Dogs

My old working dog is always admired
Even though he has retired.
His favourite job is retrieving my wellie
That I left in the kitchen while watching the tele.
With an air of pride and his find complete
He brings it back to drop at my feet.
I try to tell him his work is done
But I think he does it just for fun.
He still eagerly bounds through meadow and copse
Then on his return he lies down and flops.
Obedience to him is the name of the game
Some working dogs can put others to shame.

Our Dalmation

His nose is wet
He's full of health
And he's always very pleased with himself.
But he is covered in spots
Or are they called dots
They even look like big ink blots!
He has spots on his socks
And spots on his toes
He even has spots to the end of his nose!
If you don't like the spots on a Dalmatian
Then perhaps you should have an Alsatian!

Ode to a Faithful Friend

A faithful friend
When you're in need
Always there a friend indeed.
That sultry look with longing eyes
Will never fail to surprise.
A welcome on which you can depend
Always there is your faithful friend.
With delight they'll jump about
A happy greeting there's no doubt.
Always there and never falters
As they grow old nothing alters.
With the passing of the years
Their exuberance disappears.
Not quite so agile as they fade
But their affections you'd never trade.
Sadly, when they come to rest
You know you've always done your best
To respect their faithfulness and trust,
Another puppy .... it's a must!

Westie The Warrior

Our Westie is a warrior
He's famous down our street.
If he sees you walking
He'll chase around your feet.
If he see's you cycle
He'll run and chase your wheels
If he catches up with you
He'll nibble at your heels.
He'll have a go at anything
And always stands his ground
Which can be to his detriment
When strange dogs are around.
When our Warrior is on patrol
He likes to think he's in control.
No other dogs dare compete
When with our Warrior they meet.
There are some dogs in his gang
They run around like boomerangs.
But when it comes to having guts
They're all just soppy little mutts.
Our westie is small and his coat is white
We know his bark is worse than his bite.

Peaches the Poodle

Peaches is a snooty poodle
Her favourite food is chicken with noodle.
She wins at all the posh dog shows
She really is a great big pose.

The fluffy top knot on her head
Has ribbons in it blue and red.
She stands alert with tail erect
She knows she has not one defect.

She can tell just at a glance
The other dogs don't stand a chance.
Her coat is curly and pale pink
The 'Queen of Poodles' so she thinks.

She gives a smile and preens and prances
As round the ring she trots and dances.
The other dogs are in despair
But Peaches, she just doesn't care.

Then along came the big dog 'Slink'
Who saw a bottle of black ink
On the judges' table top
Then he knew he couldn't stop.

He pawed the table as he passed
The ink fell to the floor so fast.
Slink didn't care cause he was black
Or even if he'd get a smack.

Poor Peaches got a big surprise
As she began to realise
Her colour was no longer pink
Her coat was coloured by the ink.

She was absolutely horrified
Because she wasn't identified.
"Who is this dog?" someone called
The old judge was so appalled.

How the other dogs did laugh
When someone took a photograph.
Peaches ran away to hide
She couldn't see the funny side.

She was so alone and quite ashamed
As this time, first prize wasn't claimed!

Howard at the Vets

I trapped my paw inside the door
And it became so very sore.
I had to go to see the vet
Along with all the other pets.
There we were, all in a line
Waiting our turn one at a time.
Some pets were big and some were small
And some you could hardly see at all.
We don't enjoy our visits here
Sometimes we're scared and full of fear.
He called my name. "It's you next Howard."
Oh! I wish it didn't rhyme with coward.
"Show me your paw" the nice vet said.
"Oh! deary me, it's gone quite red."
He made me sit so very still
I looked at him and felt quite ill.
He prodded and pushed, I nearly had a fit
But to my surprise, it didn't hurt one bit.

He said I hadn't misbehaved
And that I'd been so very brave.
Outside people gathered round
I hope my bandage won't come unwound!
Oh! poor boy, he's hurt his foot
We trust it wasn't a very deep cut.
I drew a sympathetic crowd
With my bandage - I felt quite proud.

Weimaraner

Maud was a Weimaraner
There is no dog you would find calmer.
Sleek and silver grey is she
A beautiful colour you must agree.
Her coat to the touch is very like silk
Short and soft as smooth as milk.
Quietly she treads and silently trots
Her feet sound cushioned as she gently plods.
With mournful eye she'll look you over
Looking longingly at you on the sofa.
She'll nudge and push to get on your knee
Saying "Hey make room for me!"
"That's my place, so, come on, move over
I'm Maud Weimaraner, not that boisterous Rover!"

Pointers

Paw in the air is the Pointer's stance
Recognisable at a glance.
Sensitive smell
Just as well.
Mouth warm and soft
Head held aloft.
Snif, snifs the air
What's over there?
Patiently and silent stands
Waiting for his master's commands.
He is also trained to obey
From his master's side he will not stray.
When he gets home he bounds over the gate
He's enjoyed his day and thinks life's great.

Hearing Dogs

Hearing dogs come in all shapes and sizes
As they train they will win prizes.
They love their work, it's like a game
First they're taught to know their name.
They learn to listen for the bell
And the telephone as well.
They'll lie with one ear to the ground
To listen for the slightest sound.
Because their owners cannot hear
They like to keep their dogs quite near,
So when the doorbell goes ring, ring
Or when the kettle starts to sing,
They jump upon their owners knee
To let them know it's time for tea.
They never have to speak a word
Their owners know that they have heard.
They lick their face and wag their tail
They work so hard and never fail.

German Shepherd

The German Shepherd is very brave
Once he's trained he will behave.
He'll stand on guard all through the day
And soldier like he will obey.

He'll march with the army on parade
There isn't a task he will evade.
He'll chase the man who robs and steels
And pull his arm and nip at his heels.
He'll knock a robber to the ground
Until a policeman can be found.
People watching all applaud
As he receives his just reward.

Cyber-Pets

Tamagochi is the name
Of a Cyber-pet type of game.
These pets needs, you cannot shirk
You get all of the pleasure
And none of the work.
Train it!
Feed it!
But don't mistreat it.
Walk it!
Talk to it!
You can even breed it.
Love it, and tender to it's every need
Is a digital friend a friend indeed?
Clean it!
Play with it!
Sing it a song
Oh, dear this time
I've got it wrong.
This pet, you can even take to bed
This digital playmate is taxing my head.
When the time comes, it'll say goodbye
It doesn't matter how hard you try.
But, it will come back another day
To let you have another play.
A "do it yourself" dog comes in a kit
But this one won't make you healthy and fit.
A techno pet!
Well, it's alright!
But a real dog is a true delight.

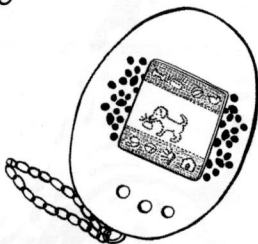

Doggy's Day Out

I think it's today
We're going away.
The car is packed with buckets and spades
A picnic and some lemonades.
The children shout "I think that's all."
Oh! No! it's not. "Where's my ball?"
I saw them pack my dish and bone
So I know I won't be left alone.
Oh! what fun it's going to be
Make sure you leave some space for me.
I've never seen the sea before
I can't wait to dip in my paw.
I'll help build castles in the sand
Perhaps we'll listen to a band.
I'll chase the waves as they come for me
And go for a boat ride on the sea.
When I hear them say the day is done
It's time for off you've had your fun
I sit upon my owner's knee
So through the window I can see.
I fall asleep and have a dream
That I've just had a giant ice cream.
"Will we be home in time for tea?"
"Was I the first to see the sea?"

Ye Olde Spaniel

I'm a King Charles Spaniel
I am a Cavalier!
I'd Chase off those Roundheads
If they were here.

I feel very regal
As I sit in my chair.
I bark commands at those who pass
But they don't seem to care.

What's the point in being royal
If you can't have your way?
Why should I be the one
Who has to sit and stay?

Mollie the Collie

Mollie the Collie lives on a farm
She makes sure the sheep come to no harm.
She has a glossy coat she's black and white.
She guards the sheep with all her might.

When the lambs come out to play
She watches them dance their jumping ballet.
She rounds them up into their pen
And counts them in one to ten.

But where's the black one? He must be found
Oh! there he is playing merry go round.
She stays awake all through the night
If a fox came she'd give it a fright.

Next morning it is market day
The shepherd's whistle she'll obey.
She rounds them up from hill and glen
But where's the black one? He's gone again!

She finds him in a bale of straw
And returns him to the flock once more.

The Basset Hound

Melting eyes and big wet nose
This is a verse I must compose.
Great long ears that sweep the ground
It has to be a Basset Hound.
He struts along with tail aloft
His tummy full and round and soft.
When he barks it is a bay
That can be heard from miles away.
It's always very fascinating
To watch him scent out everything.
That nose of his just never stops
He once sniffed out our mutton chops.
It's sniff, snort, snort, sniff
I think he needs a handkerchief.
When he sleeps there is no repose
His lungs are working like bellows.
He can even sniff smells in his dreams
You'd think his lungs would run out of steam.

Horace

My name is Horace and I'm sure you'll agree
I'm certainly not a pedigree.
I'm a bit of this and a bit of that
But at least, I'm not a cat!
I'm black and tan with four white feet
A bushy tail makes me complete.
I love to play with squeaky toys
And anything that makes a noise.
I'm great at heading big balloons
Sometimes they burst and Grandma swoons!
I chase the squirrels in the park
I only do it for a lark!
If there is no one else around
I sneak into the kids playground.
I climb the steps to the top of the slide
And slither down on my backside.
I gallop home in time for tea
And bark I'm back! Did you miss me?

Sam's Bath Time

I can hear her laugh
As she brings out the bath.
There's the doggy shampoo
And the brush and comb too.
She'll be finding the scissors
And a pair of the clippers.
I rush up the stairs
And make myself scarce.
I hide under the bed
And pretend to be dead.
But she's made up her mind
Why is she so unkind?
She knows where I am
And shouts "Come on Sam,
You know we'll have fun
There's no need to run."

I'm submerged in the water
The shampoo's all a lather.
She sings "Rub a dub dub
My Sam's in the tub."
Then comes a towel
I begin to howl.

But soon it's all over
And I smell like fresh clover.
Then she trims my long hair
Leaving plenty to spare
And clips my long nails
"Keep still," she wails.
At last it is done
And I'm put down to run.
She says "There that wasn't so bad
You've been a very good lad!"

Puppies

Six little puppies born in the night
Six little puppies with eyes shut tight.
Three little boys and three little girls
Two had funny tails just like curls.
As soon as I saw them I was spellbound
Their tummies were soft and warm and round.
They had tiny noses that felt like silk
They whimpered as they suckled their mothers milk.
I watched them growing from day to day
And as their eyes opened they began to play.
Their favourite game was rough and tumble
Ending up in a great big jumble.
They were into this and into that
Then they all fell asleep in my big straw hat.
It was better than tele when I came home from school,
But homework first - that was the rule.
When I had finished there was plenty of time
To play with my puppies and write this rhyme.

Bess

I have a dog
Her name is Bess
Her coat is always in a mess.
No matter how
I brush and comb
It's in a tangle
When she gets home.
I wring my hands in deep despair
As I look around at all the hair.
I use a spray to tease the tugs
I know it hurts
As I comb her lugs.
But when I've done
She looks a treat
And for two minutes
She looks so neat.
But then she'll shake
Oh! what a horror
Goodness knows just why I bother.
I suppose it's cos I love her lots
Even down to those hairy knots.

Sparky the Wire-haired Terrier

A wire haired terrier ran amock
And gave himself an electric shock!
He really was a silly mug.
When he went to investigate the plug.

His four short legs were all a shiver
His hair on end and tail a quiver!
Now we know from his little game
How the terrier got its name!

Nathaniel the Spaniel

Floppy ears and cold wet nose
Curly coat right down to his toes.
Sometimes black and sometimes brown
With cute little legs not far from the ground.
What's so special about Nathaniel?
He's just a lively, loveable, loyal, spaniel.

Impatience

I yawn and stretch
As I've slept all night
Another day
And it's getting light.

I bark, wake up
Or you'll be late
I want my walk
And I can't wait!

I run and jump
Upon the bed
I pull and tug
At the bedspread.

Can we go
To the woods today?
Will there be time
For me to play?

Will we go out
In the car?
If we do
Will it be far?

I heard them moan
And then a grumble
As I played
My rough and tumble.

Come on! Come on!
The sun is out
This is what
Life's all about.

I try wet licks
On sleepyheads
At last it's worked
They're out of bed.

When they come down
I'm by the door
Like any well trained
Labrador!

Massive the Great Dane

Massive is a huge Great Dane
Who does not like it in the rain.
He will not put a paw outside
So under the table he tries to hide.
Hasn't he got any pride?
He really looks undignified.
He's very glad he stayed indoors
And hides his head beneath his paws.
He is so strong and won't be moved
Until the weather has improved.
He cannot fit into the car
If he gets in he looks bizarre.
He has to stand upon the seat
Co's there's nowhere else to put his feet!
We have to wind the windows down
Massive looks just like a clown.
With long tongue hanging from his mouth
His head is North and his tail is South!
We'll have to buy a bigger car
So Massive won't stick out so far
And even buy a bigger house
Instead of Massive, I should have a mouse!

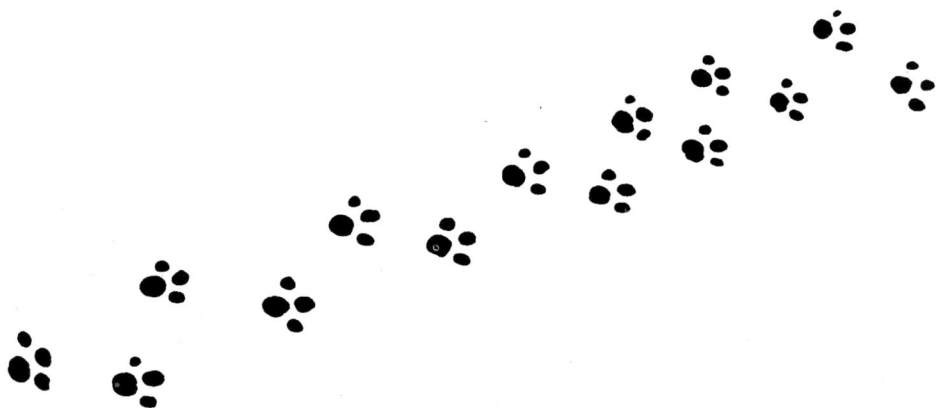